J745.5 P (P/T)

Smart Kids
Activity

priddy books
big ideas for little people

Contents

What you need   4
Supplies for creative activities

Animal masks   6
Creative creature disguises

Tissue pom-poms   9
Celebrate a special occasion

Paper roses   10
Make some pretty paper flowers

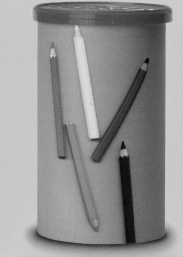

Note to parents

This book is full of creative ideas that will help you make the most of the spare time that you spend with your children. These activities will ease the boredom of a rainy day spent indoors, and encourage your child's creativity and imagination.

Scented pillows   12
Make a sweet-smelling present

Scanner art   14
Use a computer to decorate your things

Rainbow crayons   16
Melt crayons into big rainbow coloring blocks

Friendship tree   17
Show your friends and family on a special tree

This edition copyright © 2010 St. Martin's Press, LLC
175 Fifth Avenue, New York, NY 10010.
Originally published as My Big Creative Activity Book
copyright © 2004

Created for St. Martin's Press by
priddy☺books

Desk organizer   18
Keep your desk neat and tidy

Book covers   20
Brighten up your old textbooks

Paper people   22
Colorful paper characters

Cupcake creations   24
Decorate cupcakes for special occasions

Friendship necklaces 26
Special jewelry for you and
your best friend

Pasta jewelry 27
Fashion fun with food

Valentine heart bag 28
A special gift for Valentine's Day

Bird feeders 30
Attract birds to your yard or terrace

Pebble caterpillar 32
Make a 10-legged rocky creature

Mini desert 34
Create your own desert garden

Herb garden 36
Grow a pot full of flavors for
the kitchen

Marbled eggs 38
Decorate eggs for a colorful Easter

Pressed flowers 40
Decorative ideas with pressed petals

Easter pictures 42
Draw some cute Easter pictures

Creepy candies 43
Chocolate ghosts for Halloween

Halloween pumpkins 44
Learn how to light up your
house at Halloween

Pumpkin lanterns 46
More creative ideas for your
pumpkins

Jelly jar lantern 48
Make a colorful glowing lantern

Halloween pictures 49
Some spooky things to draw
for Halloween

Pom-pom wreath 50
A seasonal snowball decoration

Potato print gift wrap 51
Design your own wrapping paper

Cookie stars 52
Shiny, candy-filled cookies

Candy tree 54
Decorate your Christmas tree
with treats

Celebration cookies 56
Sweet festive treats

Snowflakes 58
Bring a white Christmas indoors

Christmas pictures 61
Draw your own Christmas pictures

Wizard hat 62
Make and decorate a wizard hat

Wizard wand 63
Grant wishes and make magic

Index 64

What you need

Supplies for creative activities

Getting started

The activities in this book use things you can find at home, or that can be bought from art supply stores. Some of the most commonly-used materials are shown here, but always check the 'You will need' section at the start of each activity before you start.

Chopping board

Paints

Cookie cutters

Spoon

Glass bowls

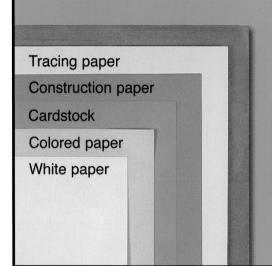
Tracing paper
Construction paper
Cardstock
Colored paper
White paper

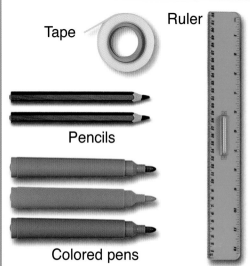
Tape
Ruler
Pencils
Colored pens

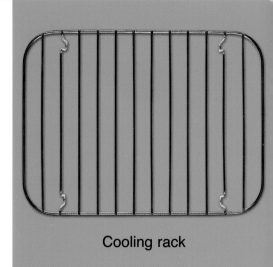
Cooling rack

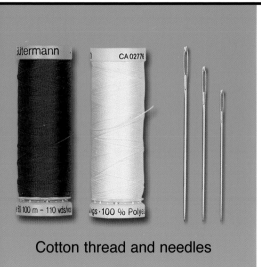
Cotton thread and needles

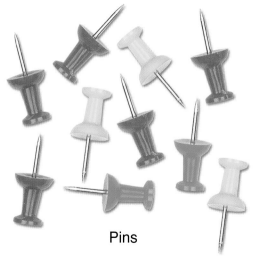
Pins

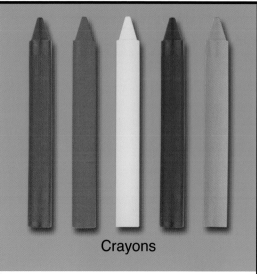
Crayons

Mini muffin pan

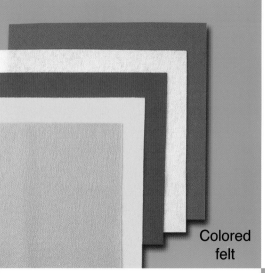
Colored felt

Compasses

Pinking shears

Scissors

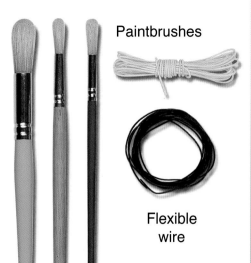
Glue

String

Paintbrushes

Flexible wire

Safety first

Children will be able to complete many of the activities in this book by themselves, but some of them will require adult supervision and assistance. We have made it clear which things should be done specifically by an adult.

Animal masks

Creative creature disguises

You will need:

- colored felt
- construction paper
- scissors • pencil
- tracing paper
- paintbrush
- elastic • needle
- glue • pen
- templates supplied

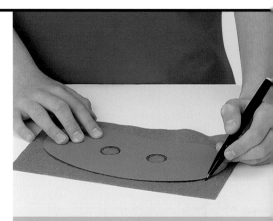

1 Trace the eyepiece template onto construction paper and cut out. Copy this onto a piece of felt.

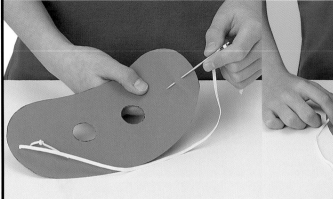

2 Cut a length of elastic to fit around your head. Make holes in the eyepiece and attach the elastic.

3 Cut out the felt shape and glue it to the construction paper eyepiece.

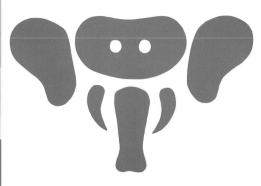

4 Trace the templates of your choice from pages 7 or 8 to make the rest of your chosen mask.

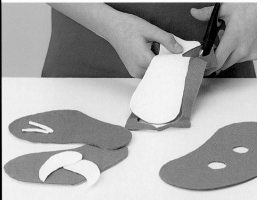

5 Copy the shapes onto felt and cut them out.

6 Glue the felt shapes onto the construction paper pieces.

7 Glue the shapes together to make the masks. Look at the finished masks to see how.

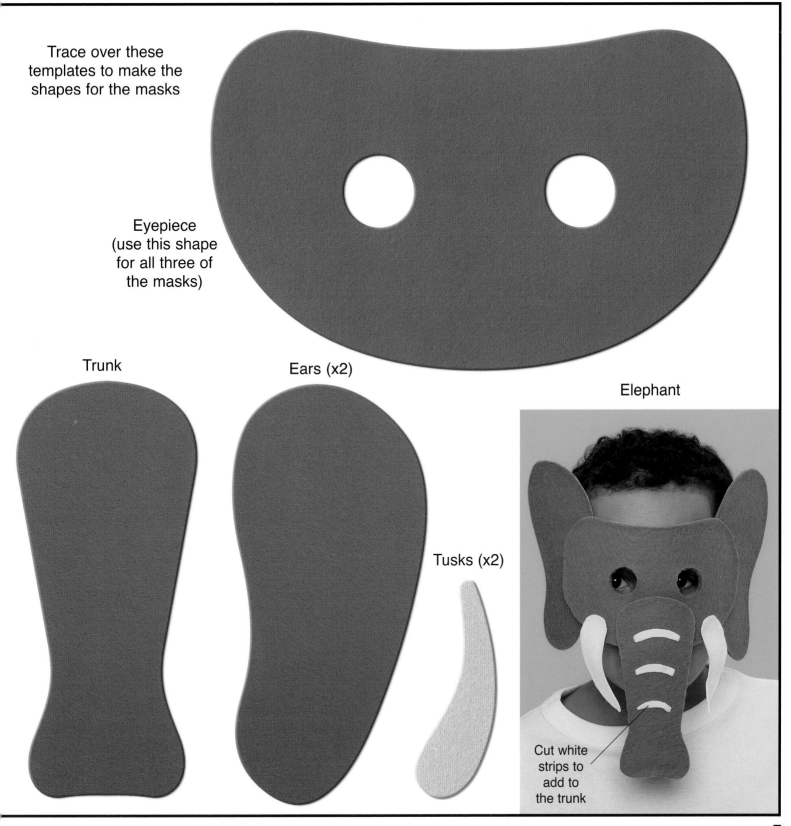

Trace over these templates to make the shapes for the masks

Eyepiece (use this shape for all three of the masks)

Trunk

Ears (x2)

Tusks (x2)

Elephant

Cut white strips to add to the trunk

7

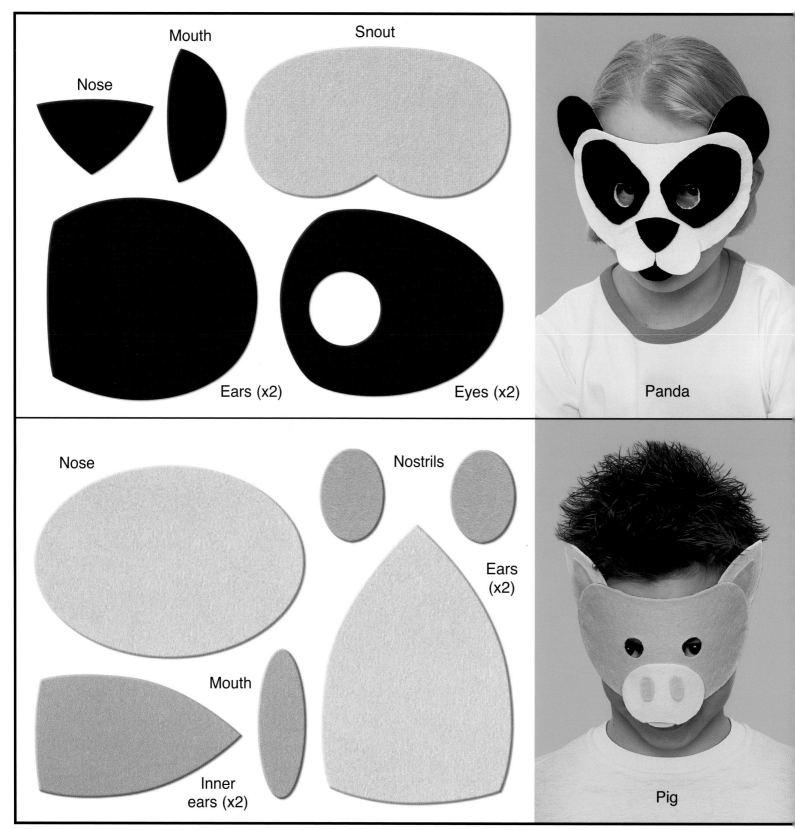

Nose

Mouth

Snout

Ears (x2)

Eyes (x2)

Panda

Nose

Nostrils

Ears (x2)

Mouth

Inner ears (x2)

Pig

8

Tissue pom-poms

A fun way to celebrate a special occasion

You will need:

- at least 18 sheets of tissue paper (various colors)
- lollipop sticks
- scissors
- tape

Do not cut all the way

1 Place three sheets of tissue paper together. Fold in half lengthwise and cut 1-inch wide strips as shown.

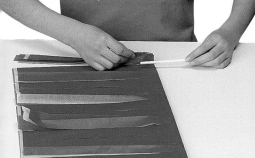

2 Starting at one end, roll the folded edge around the end of the lollipop stick and secure with tape.

Remember to secure each tissue strip to the stick with tape

3 Repeat three more times per pom-pom, wrapping each new tissue strip around the previous one.

4 These pom-poms are perfect for celebrating sports day, birthdays and all kinds of special occasions. They are also great for practicing to be a cheerleader!

Paper roses

Make some pretty paper flowers

1 Cut a 6-inch piece of flexible wire. Add a piece of cotton wool to one end and glue yellow paper around it.

2 Fold the yellow paper in half crosswise, then fold it the same way three more times.

3 Draw a curve around the edge of the paper as shown. Cut around it and unfold the paper.

4 Wrap the petals around the wire and tie cotton thread around the base of the flower.

5 Cut leaf shapes from the green paper. Glue a 3-inch piece of flexible wire between two shapes.

6 Make three to four leaves in this way. Wind the leaf wires around the rose stem.

7 Cover the stem and the leaf wires with a strip of green paper. Glue the end of the paper in place.

These paper roses make
a wonderful springtime
decoration or Mother's Day gift

Scented pillows

Make a sweet-smelling present

You will need:

- 8-inch x 4-inch piece of white felt
- 3-inch x 3-inch piece of pink felt
- lavender or similar dried, scented flowers
- scissors • ribbon
- sewing needle
- cotton thread
- fabric glue

1 Cut the white felt in half crosswise. Cut the pink felt into a heart shape.

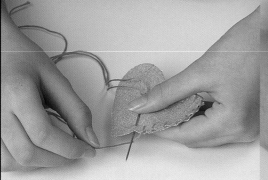

2 Sew around the edge of the heart for decoration. Glue it to one of the white squares.

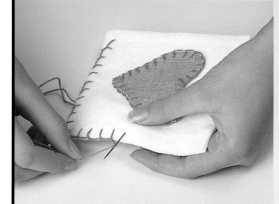

3 Place the two white squares together and sew around three sides, leaving one open.

4 Fill the bag with the lavender. Place a piece of ribbon in one corner to make a loop and secure it in place with fabric glue. Sew up the remaining side of the pillow.

Try different fabrics

Or the first letter of a name

A pretty flower

Or a Valentine's gift?

13

Scanner art

Use a computer to decorate your things

You will need:

- computer
- scanning software
- scanner • color printer
- colored paper • ruler
- storage containers
- objects to scan
- paintbrush
- glue • scissors

1 Choose the objects that you wish to scan and the color of paper you would like to use.

2 Choose a container for the objects. Measure it and make a note of its size.

3 Place the objects on the scanner. Put the paper above them and scan them into your computer.

4 Check that the size of the image is big enough to cover the container you are using.

5 Print out your picture in color. Make sure that you are happy with it.

6 Cut out the picture to the correct size if necessary.

7 Carefully glue the picture to the container. You might need an adult to help you.

Why not try some of these designs?

Chalk sticks

Colored pencils

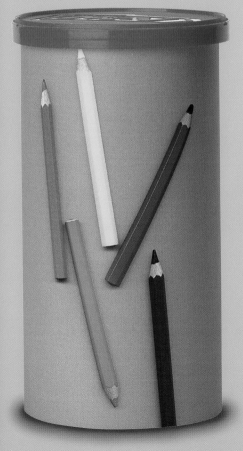

Toy cars

Magnetic numbers

Rainbow crayons

Melt crayons into big rainbow coloring blocks

You will need:

- old colored crayons
- chopping board
- cooling rack
- kitchen knife
- mini muffin pan

1 Ask an adult to cut the crayons into ½-inch long pieces.

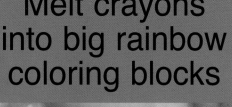

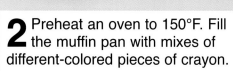

2 Preheat an oven to 150°F. Fill the muffin pan with mixes of different-colored pieces of crayon.

3 Bake for 8 to 9 minutes or until the wax has melted. Allow them to cool and take them out of the pan.

4 If you find that it is difficult to get them out, place them in a freezer for around an hour – they should pop out. You can use your rainbow crayons to quickly produce wonderful multicolored pictures.

Friendship tree

Show your friends and family on a tree

You will need:

- leaves for all the people you would like to include
- glue • pen
- an old heavy book (such as a telephone directory)
- a big piece of white paper
- 3 large pieces of brown construction paper
- scissors

1 Collect some pretty, colored leaves. Lay them flat between the pages of a heavy book overnight.

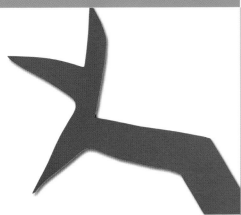

2 Make a brown paper tree with enough branches for your friends and your close family.

Name

3 Make labels for each person you are going to put on your tree, and stick one label to each leaf.

Joe
John
Dan
Sarah
Nicole
Sam
Beth
Adam
Ben
Brad
Maria
Alex
Mom
Jack
Julie
Scott
Kerry
Dad
Me

4 Stick your own leaf at the bottom of the tree, then add all of the other leaves to the branches. Why not make new branches as you make new friends and your family grows?

Desk organizer

Keep your desk neat and tidy

You will need:

- piece of strong fabric
- pieces of colored felt
- cotton thread
- sewing needle • ruler
- scissors • buttons
- fabric eyelet kit • iron
- iron-on adhesive tape
- stick-on plastic hooks

1 Cut out a piece of fabric, 19 inches long by 12 inches wide.

2 Fold in 1 inch on all four sides. Ask an adult to iron the hems down with the iron-on adhesive tape.

3 Ask an adult to fit an eyelet about 1 inch in from the corners of the long side.

4 Cut out different colored pieces of felt to make big pockets. Use pinking shears if you wish.

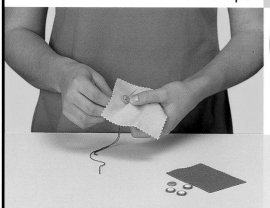

5 For pockets with flaps, cut out a piece of felt for the pocket and a triangle-shaped piece for the flap.

6 Cut a slit in the flap to make a buttonhole. Sew a button onto the pocket.

7 Sew the pockets onto the fabric in the positions that you like.

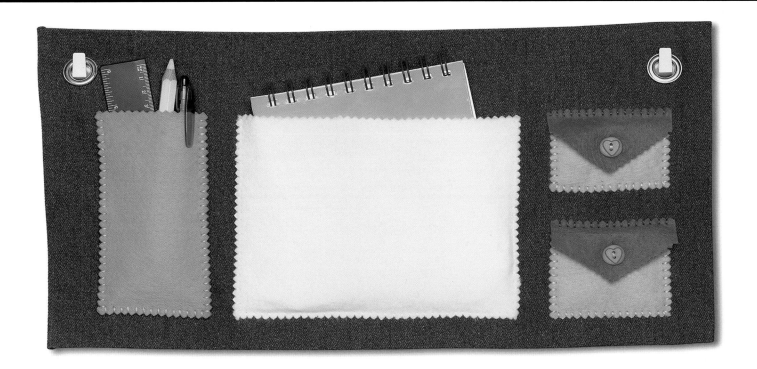

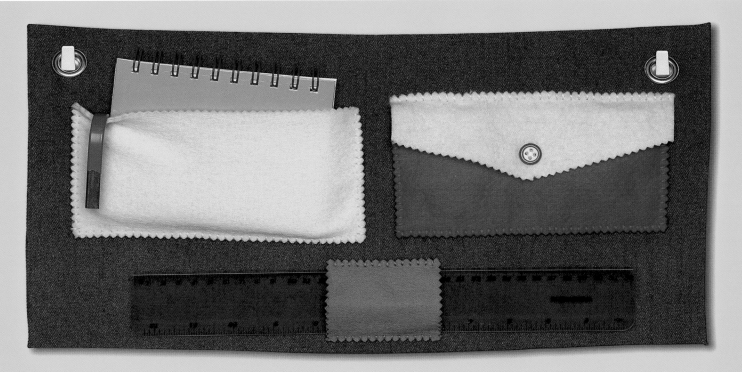

8 Stick two hooks on a wall near your desk the same distance apart as the eyelets. Hang your desk organizer on the hooks and put your stationery in the pockets. Your desk need never be in a mess again!

Book covers

Brighten up your textbooks

You will need:

- books to cover
- colored or patterned paper (pieces should be 2 inches bigger than the book on all sides)
- scissors
- glue
- stickers

1 Place the book in the center of the paper. Fold the paper against the top and bottom edges.

2 Place the closed book on the folded paper, 2 inches from one side. Fold the paper around one cover.

3 Remove the book and fold crisply. Slide the cover into the fold, close and then fold the other side.

4 Fold the creases neatly and slide the other cover into the sleeve. Now the book is ready to decorate. Use some stickers, or glue on some pieces of colored paper.

This is the completed cover with a polka dot design.

Glue strips of elastic to the inside of the cover and use them to hold a notebook on the outside.

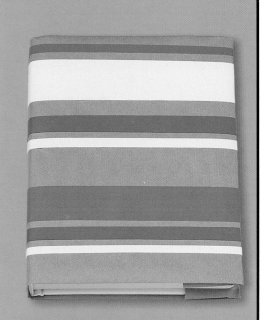

Glue colored strips to some plain paper, then use it to make a striped cover.

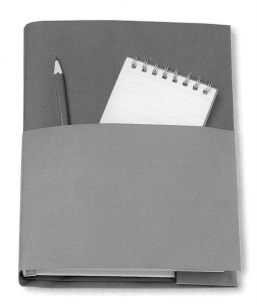

Make a half-size second cover to create a paper sleeve to store notebooks, pens or pencils.

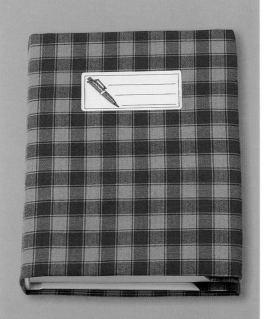

You could try using a piece of fabric as a cover. Use fabric glue to secure the folds inside.

Pictures cut from magazines or colorful stickers make good decorations for your covers.

Paper people

Make some fantastic paper characters

You will need:

- 16-inch x 12-inch sheet of red construction paper
- 2 x 8-inch x 8-inch sheets of green construction paper
- sheets of yellow, brown and orange construction paper
- scissors • pen
- glue • tape

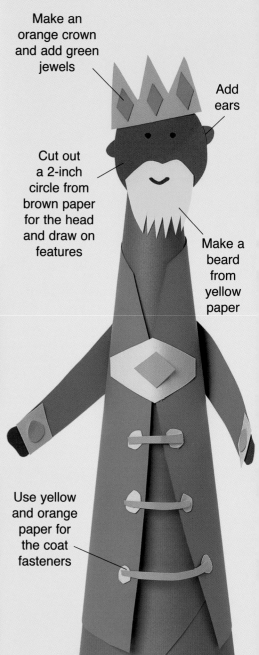

Make an orange crown and add green jewels

Add ears

Cut out a 2-inch circle from brown paper for the head and draw on features

Make a beard from yellow paper

Use yellow and orange paper for the coat fasteners

Christmas King

1 To make a Christmas King, roll the red paper into a cone. Secure it with a piece of tape.

2 Cut across the large end of the cone to make a base.

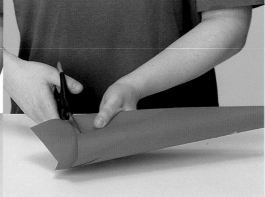

Draw this shape onto the folded paper

3 Glue one of the pieces of green paper to the cone. Fold the other piece in half, and cut out the shape.

4 Glue the shape that you have just cut out to the back of the cone as shown.

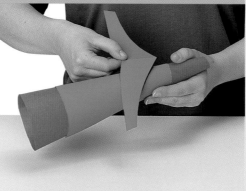

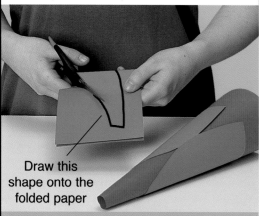

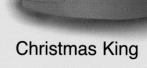

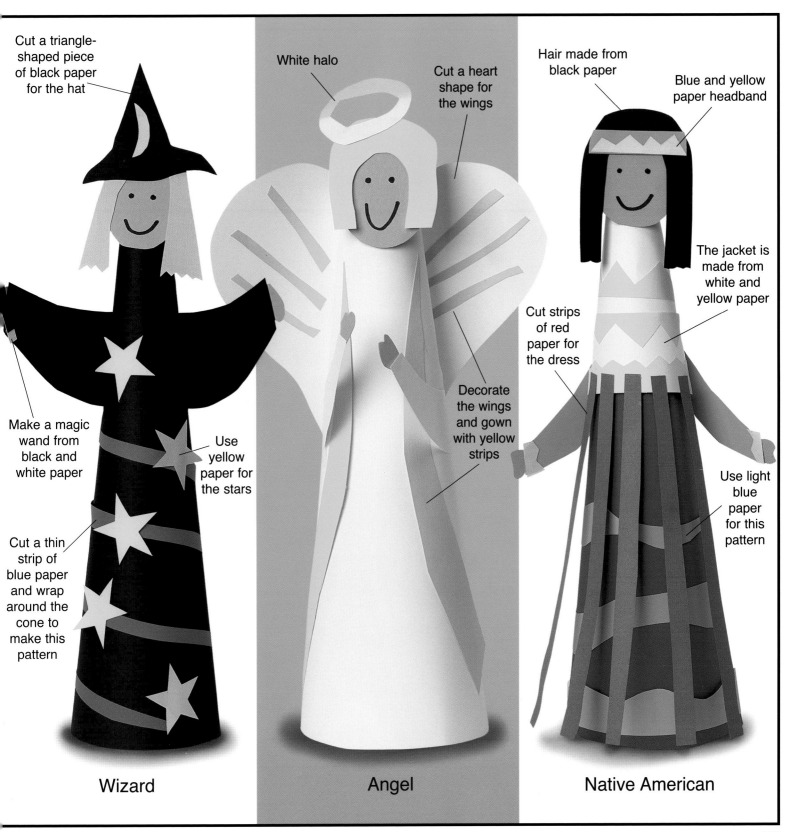

Cut a triangle-shaped piece of black paper for the hat

White halo

Cut a heart shape for the wings

Hair made from black paper

Blue and yellow paper headband

The jacket is made from white and yellow paper

Make a magic wand from black and white paper

Use yellow paper for the stars

Cut strips of red paper for the dress

Decorate the wings and gown with yellow strips

Cut a thin strip of blue paper and wrap around the cone to make this pattern

Use light blue paper for this pattern

Wizard

Angel

Native American

Cupcake creations

Decorate cupcakes for special occasions

You will need:

- ready-made cupcake mix
- 16 oz confectioners' sugar
- 6 tablespoons butter
- candies for decoration
- food coloring • mixing bowl
- cupcake liners
- mini muffin pan
- spoon • whisk
- cooling rack

1 Mix the cupcake mixture in a bowl according to the instructions on the box.

2 Spoon the mixture into the cupcake liners.

3 Bake the cupcakes as instructed on the box. Leave them to cool on a cooling rack.

4 Whisk the sugar, butter and a few drops of food coloring together to make the icing.

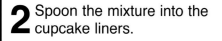

5 Ice the cupcakes using a spoon. You could decorate cupcakes using different colors of icing.

6 Use your favorite candies to decorate the cupcakes.

7 Try different designs and colors for special occasions – see the opposite page for some ideas.

Snowman

Jelly candy pieces

Two marshmallows

Valentine heart

Sugar-coated chocolate candies

Chocolate celebrations

Chocolate stars

Gone fishing

Drinking straw

Dental floss

Jelly candy fish

American flag

Jelly candy stripes

Flower

Lollipop

Jelly candy leaf

Marshmallow heart

Marshmallow

Baseball

Jelly sweet laces

Holly and berries

Jelly candy leaves

Sugar-coated chocolates

Friendship necklaces

Special jewelry for you and your best friend

You will need:

- colored beads
- thin elastic string
- scissors
- oven-bake clay
- flexible wire
- heart-shaped cookie cutter
- pinking shears
- sewing needle

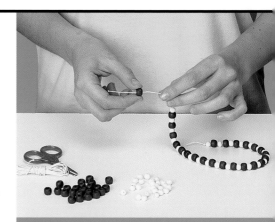

1 Thread the beads onto a length of elastic string a little longer than you need, then tie the ends.

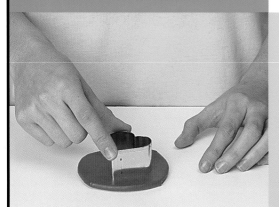

2 Knead a piece of clay until it is soft. Flatten it to about ¼-inch thick, and cut out a heart shape.

3 Cut the heart using pinking shears. Write 'best friends' across both halves with a needle.

4 Make small holes in the top of each half of the heart. Bake them for 6-8 minutes in an oven heated to 275°F and leave to cool. Attach the halves to the necklaces using pieces of flexible wire.

Pasta jewelry

Fashion fun with food

You will need:

- thin elastic string
- scissors
- beads
- pasta bows
- pasta tubes
- strips of ribbon

1 Cut the lengths of elastic string for your bracelets and necklaces a little longer than you need.

2 Decide on a design and thread the elastic string through the pasta shapes and beads. Tie the ends.

3 Tie strips of ribbon to the pasta bows for extra decoration.

4 We have created two designs as an example of what you can do – why not try some of your own? Pasta jewelry makes a great gift, or you can use it when you are dressing up!

Valentine heart bag

Make a special gift for Valentine's Day

You will need:

- 8-inch x 3-inch piece of red felt
- 8-inch x 3-inch piece of white felt
- 2 x 3-inch pieces of ribbon
- scissors
- fabric glue

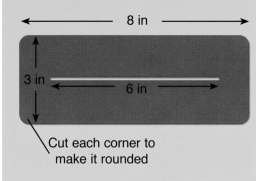

8 in

3 in

6 in

Cut each corner to make it rounded

1 Fold the red felt in half crosswise and cut a 3-inch slit along the middle (this makes a 6-inch slit).

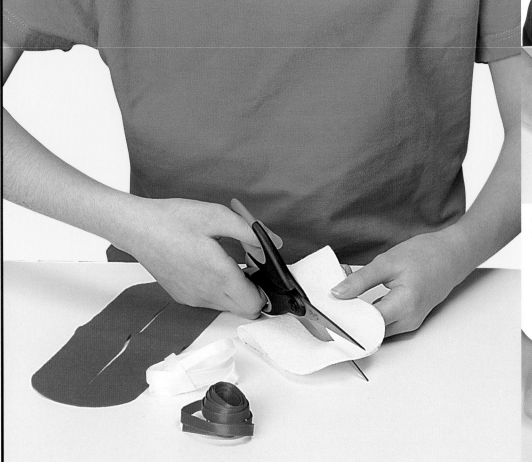

2 Next, do exactly the same with the piece of white felt as shown above.

3 Place the pieces as shown. Note the labels of each strip.

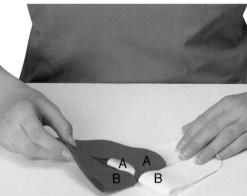

4 Slide white strip A through red strip A.

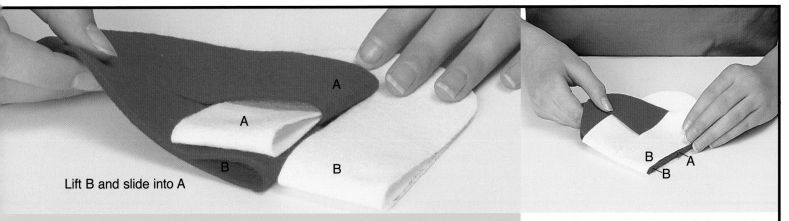

Lift B and slide into A

5 Pull white strip A until it is on top of red strip B. Then slide red strip B into white strip A.

6 Pull red strips A and B into white strip B.

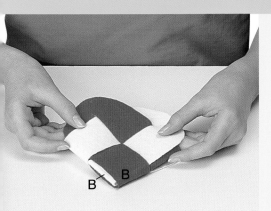

7 Slide white strip B into red strip B.

8 Finally, glue the two pieces of ribbon to the insides of the heart in two separate loops as shown.

You can fill your Valentine heart bag with delicious chocolates or pretty flowers

Bird feeders

Attract birds to your yard or terrace

You will need:

- scraps of food, such as breadcrumbs, cheese, cooked rice or vegetables
- birdseed • lard • peanuts
- mixing bowl • saucepan
- plastic cup • small twig
- large pine cone • large needle
- scissors • spoon • drill
- string • small log • hook

1 Mix the scraps with some birdseed and nuts in a bowl. Ask an adult to melt the lard in a saucepan.

2 Add the melted lard to the mixture and stir it all together with the spoon.

3 Put some of the mixture into the plastic cup and push a twig into the middle. Leave it to set.

4 Pull the mixture out of the cup and roll it in some birdseed. Tie a piece of string to the twig.

5 To make a pine cone feeder, simply push the mixture between the gaps in a pine cone.

6 To make a peanut kebab, use a needle to thread string through peanut shells and balls of mixture.

7 To make a log feeder, ask an adult to drill holes in a small log and fill them with the mixture.

This feeder is made using a gourd. You could use a small pumpkin or a melon

Peanut kebab

Plastic cup feeder

Log feeder

Pine cone feeder

8 Hang out your bird feeders and see how many birds fly by to feed!

Pebble caterpillar

Make a 10-legged rocky creature

You will need:

- 6 smooth, rounded pebbles
- popsicle sticks
- strong glue
- tempera or acrylic paint
- paintbrush
- 6 pipe cleaners

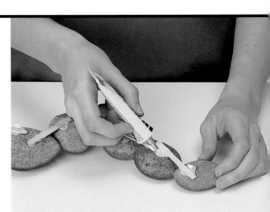

1 Arrange the pebbles in a zigzag shape. Glue popsicle sticks across them and leave to dry.

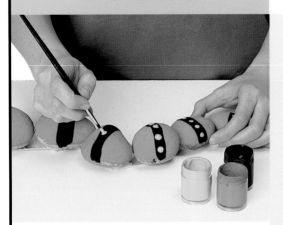

2 Carefully turn the pebbles over and paint on a caterpillar pattern. Leave the paint to dry.

3 Cut and bend the pipe cleaners to make two feelers and five pairs of legs. Glue them to the caterpillar in the positions shown above.

You could copy this pattern or create your own design. See the pictures on the opposite page for some more rock painting ideas

Stars and spirals

Hearts and flowers

Spots and stripes

How about making one of these cute bugs?

Mini desert

Create your own desert garden

You will need:

- succulents (plants with fleshy leaves and stems that store water, such as cacti)
- container (about 3 inches deep)
- gravel • compost
- decorative stones
- watering can • trowel

1 Half-fill the container, first with a thin layer of gravel, then with a layer of compost.

2 Decide how you want to arrange the plants before you take them out of their pots.

3 Remove the plants from their pots and plant them in the compost. Place decorative stones around them.

4 Water the plants lightly when you have finished. Place your mini desert in a sunny window. These plants like to dry out and then be well watered, so check that they are dry before you water them.

Jade plant

Flowering cactus

Agave

Flaming Katy

Sedum

35

Herb garden

Grow a pot full of flavors for the kitchen

You will need:

- small herb plants, such as parsley, chives, purple sage, thyme and basil
- trowel • watering can
- compost • gravel
- large container

1 Put a layer of gravel about 2 inches deep in the bottom of the container.

2 Add compost until the container is about three-quarters full.

3 Plant the herbs in the compost. Put the largest plant in the middle of the pot.

4 Push the compost down firmly around the plants, adding more if needed. Water the herbs well. Trimming or picking the herbs regularly will help them to grow and keep their flavor.

Thyme

Basil

Lemon thyme

Purple sage

Chives

Chives

Parsley

Marbled eggs

Decorate eggs for a colorful Easter

You will need:

- hard boiled eggs
- bowl or saucepan
- crayons
- cheese grater
- plate
- hot water
- thick cardboard
- tacks or pins
- spoon

1 Push tacks or pins through a piece of cardboard as shown. This is a stand for drying the eggs.

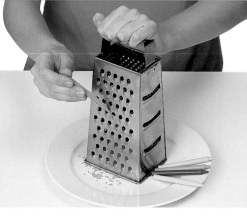

2 Peel off any labels and grate the crayons into fine pieces.

3 Ask an adult to fill a bowl with very hot water. Add the grated crayon pieces.

4 Dip an egg fully into the water using a spoon. Cover it in as much wax as you can.

5 Remove the egg slowly up through the wax. Place it on the stand and leave the wax to set.

6 Decorate as many eggs as you like in the same way using different colors of crayon. Try using mixtures of colors to get a really crazy rainbow effect.

A basket full of brightly colored eggs makes an excellent Easter decoration

Pressed flowers

Decorative ideas with pressed petals

1 Collect some flowers and leaves. Choose a varied selection of colors and types.

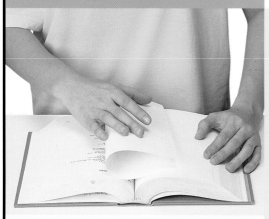

2 Fold the blotting paper in half crosswise. Open it up and place it in the center of the book.

3 Arrange the flowers and leaves flat on one side of the blotting paper, leaving space between them.

4 Carefully fold the paper, then close the book. Place more heavy books on top of it and allow the flowers and leaves to press flat and dry out. This should take about three to four weeks.

5 After that time, carefully open the blotting paper, removing the dried, pressed flowers and leaves.

6 To make gift cards, cut out pieces of construction paper on which to mount the flowers and leaves.

Tie a ribbon through the hole

7 Fold the paper, then glue the flowers and leaves on one side. Punch a hole through the corner.

Why not try making some pretty bookmarks or birthday cards?

Easter pictures

Draw some cute Easter pictures

1 For a spring flower, draw the petals in the top-right of your piece of paper.

2 Add the stem and leaves as shown. Use your favorite color for the petals.

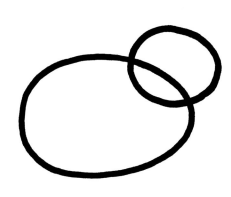

1 To draw an Easter bunny, start with two oval shapes for the body and head, as above.

2 Add the outlines of the ears, fluffy tail and feet.

3 Finally, add the details of the eyes, whiskers and toes. Finish by coloring in your bunny.

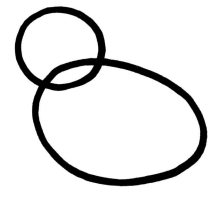

1 As with the Easter bunny, begin by drawing two oval shapes for your Easter chick.

2 Add the outlines of the beak, wings and feet.

3 Add eyes and detail to the beak, wings and feet. Give the chick fluffy feathers and color it in.

Creepy candies

Chocolate ghosts for Halloween

You will need:

- 12 oz white chocolate
- milk chocolate chips
- 1½ tablespoons vegetable oil
- heatproof bowl • saucepan
- lollipop sticks
- teaspoon
- tablespoon
- baking tray
- waxed paper

1 Ask an adult to melt the white chocolate in a bowl, over a pan of hot water. Then add the vegetable oil.

2 Put one tablespoon of chocolate onto waxed paper. Use a teaspoon to make a ghost shape.

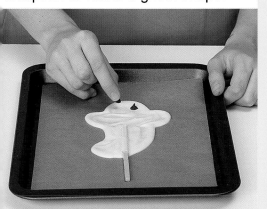

3 Add two chocolate chips for spooky eyes. Press a lollipop stick into the ghost as shown above.

4 You should be able to make about 12-15 ghosts with this mixture. Leave them to cool in the refrigerator for about five minutes, then carefully peel them off the paper. Then try some spooky designs of your own!

Halloween pumpkins

How to light up your house at Halloween

You will need:

- pumpkins
- metal spoon
- sharp knife • tape
- bowl • pen • paper
- chopping board
- pins or toothpicks
- candles and holders
- apple corer

1 Draw a face onto a pumpkin. You could copy the one shown on these pages.

2 Ask an adult to slice off the top of the pumpkin as shown.

3 Scoop out the insides of the pumpkin with a spoon.

4 Carefully cut out the pumpkin's features with a knife. Ask an adult to help you if necessary.

1 An alternative method is to draw your design on paper and stick it to the pumpkin.

2 Press through the outline using a pin or a toothpick to make small holes in the pumpkin.

3 Then use a knife to fully cut out the shape. This method is useful for more complicated shapes.

Once your design is cut out, you need to light up your Halloween pumpkin. Firstly put a candle into a holder, then place it in the pumpkin. For smaller pumpkins you could use tea lights instead. Now ask an adult to light the candle and put your pumpkin on display to spook your friends and neighbors!

Pumpkin lanterns

More creative ideas for your pumpkins

1 Use a template to mark your design onto the pumpkin as described on the previous page.

2 Make shallow cuts into the pumpkin's skin and scrape away to complete the pattern.

You could try using a melon

Use an apple corer to make these holes

This moon and stars design is ideal for Halloween

3 You could carve your house number into a pumpkin to hang outside your house. Try experimenting with designs of your own. You could even try using other fruit and vegetables too!

Why not try to make this seasonally spooky Halloween owl? The pumpkins are held together with toothpicks

Stick leaves to the top of the head

Use hazelnuts to make the eyes

Pumpkin seeds are glued to a piece of cardboard and pinned in place

The legs are made using twigs

Use long, thin leaves to make the wings

Jelly jar lantern

Make a colorful glowing lantern

You will need:

- jelly jar
- glass paint
- glass outliner paste
- paintbrush
- flexible wire
- tea light
- paper
- pencil

1 Clean the jelly jar thoroughly. Draw your design onto a piece of paper and place it inside the jar.

2 Use the outliner paste to copy the design onto the glass. Leave to dry for 24 hours.

3 Paint around your design with the glass paint. Leave this to dry for about 48 hours.

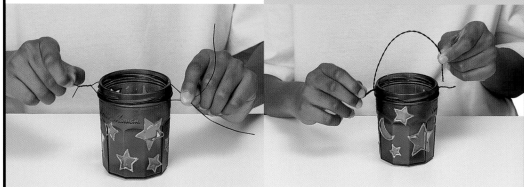

4 Tightly wrap a length of flexible wire around the rim of the jar.

5 Make a loop by attaching another length of wire to the wire around the rim.

6 Place a tea light in the jar and ask an adult to light it. All you need now is somewhere to hang it!

Halloween pictures

Some spooky things to draw for Halloween

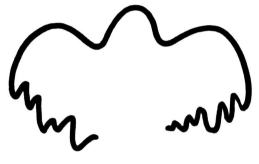

1 Start drawing a ghost by copying the squiggly shape above.

2 Finish by adding its tail and a spooky expression to its face.

1 To draw a beastly bat, copy the two oval shapes above to make its body.

2 Add some big wings and two pointed bat ears.

3 Add details to the wings and face. Then draw on its feet and color the bat in.

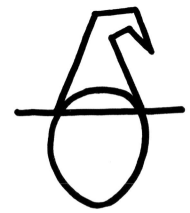

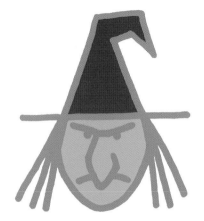

1 Draw an oval shape for a witch's face. Draw the outline of her crooked hat as shown.

2 Add her hair and a big, ugly nose.

3 Give her a really mean-looking face and then color her in.

Pom-pom wreath

A seasonal snowball decoration

You will need:

- 10-inch diameter circle of thick cardboard
- 24 x 2-inch cotton balls
- 15 x 1-inch cotton balls
- holly, or similar seasonal decorations
- glue • ruler • scissors
- pencil • compasses
- paintbrush • ribbon

1 Draw an 8-inch diameter circle on the cardboard. Ask an adult to cut it out with a pair of scissors.

2 Glue the large cotton balls onto the cardboard first, then stick the smaller ones in between.

3 Glue the decorations in place between the cotton balls. Leave the glue to set for two hours.

Hang up your wreath with a piece of ribbon

Potato print gift wrap

Design your own wrapping paper

You will need:

- large potato
- knife
- green and red paint
- paper
- blank gift tags
- chopping board
- ribbon

1 Ask an adult to cut a potato in half lengthwise.

2 Then ask an adult to help you cut out the shape of a Christmas tree in one half of the potato.

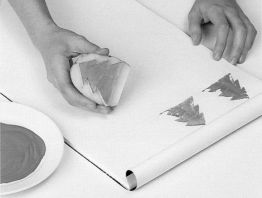

3 Press the tree shape into some green paint. Practice printing the shapes on some paper.

4 Next ask an adult to cut a shape for the Christmas tree pot in the other half of the potato.

5 Dip the pot shape into some red paint. Use it to complete your Christmas tree design.

6 Print your design onto some gift tags. Make sure you leave the paint to dry before writing on them!

Now you can wrap presents with your own design

51

Cookie stars

Shiny Christmas decorations that you can eat

You will need:

- ready-made cookie dough mixture
- selection of clear, colored hard candies • waxed paper
- non-stick baking tray
- drinking straw • star-shaped cookie cutters (2 sizes)
- rolling pin • spatula
- colored string • cooling rack

1 Make up the cookie dough according to the instructions on the box, and roll it out flat.

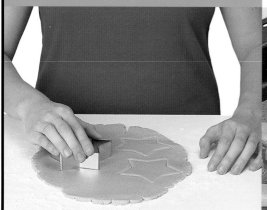

2 Cut out stars with the largest cookie cutter. Make another star inside with the smaller cutter.

3 Chop the candies into small pieces and place them in the center of the cookies.

4 Use a drinking straw to make a small hole in the top of each cookie. Bake in an oven pre-heated to the temperature shown on the cookie mixture instructions. Do not let the candy start to bubble.

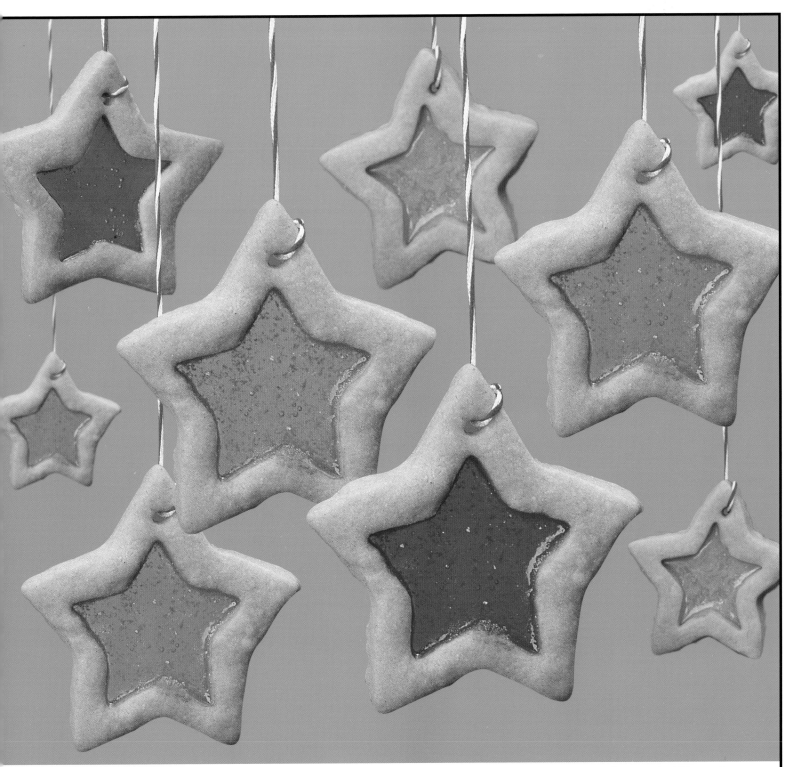

5 Carefully remove the cookies from the oven and allow them to cool thoroughly on a cooling rack. When they are cool, thread some colored string through the holes and tie them off. Now your cookies are ready to be hung on a Christmas tree – how long will you be able to resist eating them all?

Candy tree

Decorate a Christmas tree with treats

You will need:

- Christmas tree
- selection of colorful candies
- flexible wire
- thin elastic string
- sewing needle
- scissors

1 Gather together a selection of your favorite candies. Jelly types are the easiest to use.

2 To make a candy jewel decoration, take two different jelly candies.

3 Cut a 3-inch piece of flexible wire. Bend it at one end and push it through a candy.

4 Push the other candy onto the wire. Bend the top of the wire to make a hook.

1 To make a jelly bean chain, first thread a length of elastic string onto a sewing needle.

2 Thread jelly beans onto the elastic string. Vary the order of colors as you put them on.

3 When you have filled the elastic string, tie the ends to make them secure.

Hang the decorations on your tree and you have some sweet Christmas treats to eat!

Jelly bean chain

Candy jewel

Coconut candy

Celebration cookies

Decorate some sweet festive treats

You will need:

- ready-made cookie dough mixture • cookie cutters • spoon • rolling pin • waxed paper • non-stick baking tray • piping bag and attachments • confectioners' sugar • palette knife • food coloring • mixing bowl • cooling rack • cake decorations

1 Make the cookie dough according to the instructions on the box, and roll it out flat.

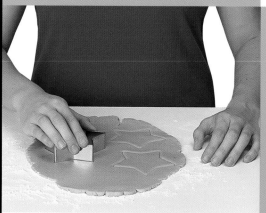

2 Use cookie cutters to make shapes, or try cutting your own shapes with the help of an adult.

3 Place them on waxed paper, on a baking tray. Bake according to the mixture instructions.

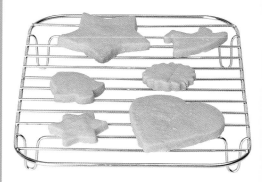

4 Carefully remove the cookies from the tray and leave them to cool on a cooling rack.

5 Make the icing according to the instructions on the box. Add your choice of food coloring.

6 Use the piping bag to draw an outline of icing. Leave it to set, then fill the outline with more icing.

7 Use a palette knife to spread the icing. Add any other decorations you want to the soft icing.

Holly leaf

Christmas tree

Love heart

Stars

57

Snow flakes

Bring a white Christmas indoors

You will need:

- white paper
- blue paper
- shiny paper
- tracing paper
- scissors
- ribbon
- cotton thread
- glitter
- glue

1 Cut out a 6-inch square piece of paper.

2 Fold the square in half diagonally. You should have a triangle like the one above.

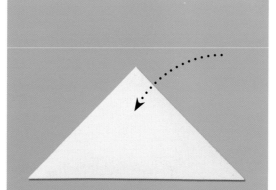

3 Fold the triangle in half so that the corners meet, as above.

4 Now you need to fold the triangle into thirds. First, fold it from left to right.

5 Then fold the opposite corner the other way, covering the first fold as shown.

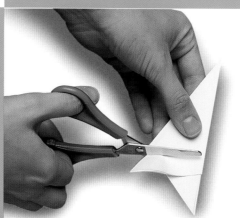

6 Cut straight across the bottom of the triangle.

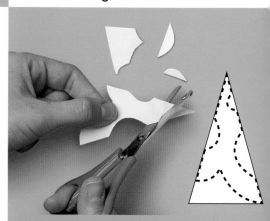

7 Carefully cut out a design. Follow the template shown here to start.

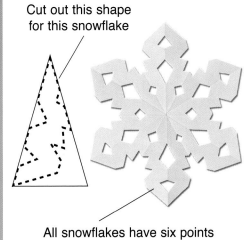

Cut out this shape for this snowflake

All snowflakes have six points

8 Unfold the paper and open the snowflake fully.

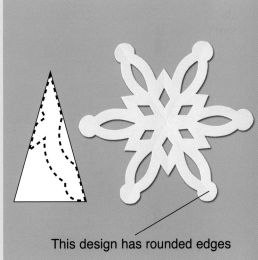

This design has rounded edges

The snowflake should look something like this

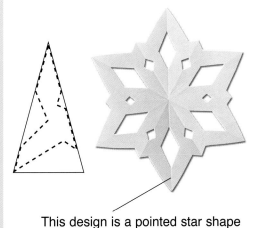

This design is a pointed star shape

Snow flakes

Creative uses for your snowflake designs

Use the snowflakes to decorate Christmas gifts

Shiny paper

How many different snowflakes can you make?

Tracing paper

Hang them on thread to make a mobile

Thread ribbon through the snowflakes to make a festive snowflake chain

Make these snowflakes using blue paper and sparkly glitter

Christmas pictures

Copy or trace these seasonal drawings

1 For holly leaves and berries, start by drawing three small circles together.

2 Add the holly leaves as above and color in the berries.

1 To draw a reindeer, start with an oval shape.

2 Add the outlines of the reindeer's nose and ears.

3 Now draw the eyes and antlers, and finish the ears. Color the nose in black.

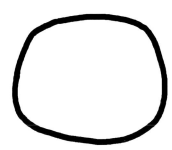

1 Give Santa Claus a big, round friendly face.

2 Next, draw his nose and the outline of his hat.

3 Finally, draw the eyes, mouth and finish the hat. Give his beard and hat bobble furry outlines.

Wizard hat

Make and decorate a wizard hat

You will need:

- 2 large pieces of construction paper
- tape
- compasses
- pencil
- scissors
- glitter paper
- glue

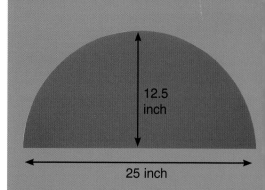

12.5 inch

25 inch

1 With the compasses, draw a large half circle on one piece of the paper, about 25 inches wide. Cut this out.

Put tape along the join

2 Fold the paper into a cone that fits around your head. Stick the cone together with tape.

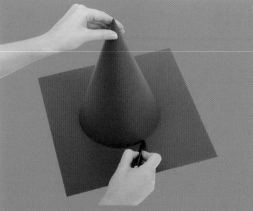

3 Place the cone onto the second piece of construction paper, and draw around it to make a circle.

4 With the compasses, draw one circle bigger than the one already drawn, and one smaller circle.

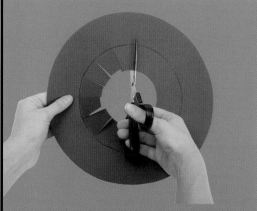

5 Cut around the largest circle, then cut out the smallest circle, to make a hole. Cut flaps as shown.

6 Turn the cone upside down, and stick the flaps to the inside of the cone with tape.

Why not make stars and moons from glitter paper?

You could also decorate your hat with stickers

Wizard wand

Grant wishes and make magic with your wand

You will need:

- small piece of white paper
- 1 piece of 8½ x 11-inch blue cardstock
- 1 piece of 8½ x 11-inch purple paper
- scissors • glue
- ruler • pencil
- double-sided tape

1 Ask an adult to draw a star shape on the white paper. Draw around it four times as shown, then cut the shapes out.

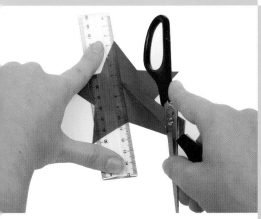

2 Use the scissors and ruler to score a line down the center of each star. Fold the stars in half along this line.

Glue here and stick to the back of this star

3 Stick the four stars together as above. Each half of each star should be glued to half of another star.

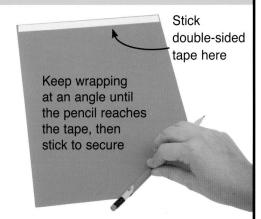

Stick double-sided tape here

Keep wrapping at an angle until the pencil reaches the tape, then stick to secure

4 For the handle, stick tape as above. Wrap the other end of the purple paper around the pencil to make a tube.

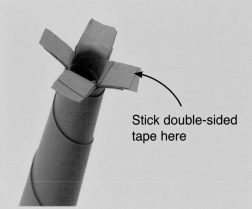

Stick double-sided tape here

5 Cut four ½-inch long slits into the top of the thin end of the handle. Bend the flaps out and stick tape.

6 Line the four flaps of the handle in between the four spaces at the bottom of the star. Stick them to the star.

You could stick glitter paper to the star

Why not attach ribbons with little stars?

Index

B

Beads …26-27
Bird feeders …30-31
Birthday cards …41
Book covers …20-21
Bookmarks …41

C

Candies …24-25, 43, 52-55, 57
Chocolate …25, 29, 43
Christmas …22-23, 25, 50-61
Computer …14-15
Cookies …52-53, 56-57
Crayons …16, 38
Cupcakes …24-25

D

Drawing …42, 49, 61

E

Easter …38-39, 42
Eggs …38-39

F

Flowers …10-13, 25, 29, 33, 40-42

G

Gift cards …41
Gift tags …51, 60

Gift wrap …51

H

Halloween …43-49
Herbs …36-37

J

Jewelry …26-27

L

Lanterns …44-46, 48
Lavender …12

M

Masks …6-8

N

Necklaces …26-27

P

Pasta …27
Pebbles …32-33
Pillows …12-13
Pipe cleaners …32-33
Plants …34-37
Pom-poms …9, 50
Potato printing …51
Pumpkins …31, 44-47

R

Rock painting …32-33

S

Snowflakes …58-60
Stationery …19-21
Stickers …20-21
Storage containers …14-15

T

Tea lights …45, 48

V

Valentines …13, 25, 28-29, 57

W

Wizards …23, 62-63